AURORA ART PUBLISHERS

LENINGRAD

PLACES OF INTEREST IN THE

Historical

and Architectural

Monuments

ENVIRONS OF LENINGRAD

Razliv

Petrodvorets

Pushkin

Lomonosov

Pavlovsk

Repino

Compiled and introduced by P. Koloskov,
I. Gurevich G. Khodasevich, V. Belanina,
L. Ivanova and E. Levenfish

Д $\frac{80103\text{-}486}{023\,(01)\text{-}75}$ без объявления

RAZLIV

The hamlet of Razliv in the vicinity of Leningrad is world famous. It was here, in this part of the Karelian Isthmus, that Lenin hid to escape arrest by agents of the Provisional government in the summer and autumn of 1917.

Lenin was compelled to go underground after the events of July in Petrograd. In the beginning of July 1917 the workers, soldiers and sailors of the capital, indignant over the anti-democratic policies of the Provisional government, took spontaneously to the streets to demand the transfer of power into the hands of the Soviets (Councils of Workers' and Soldiers' Deputies). The Bolshevik Party, anxious to impart an organized, peaceful character to the mass movement, decided to head the manifestation. Nevertheless, on July 4 the demonstration was fired on by Cossacks and cadets acting on direct orders from the government. In the wake of this bloodshed a political crisis arose, and the situation in the country changed abruptly. The peaceful period in the development of the revolution was over; the Provisional government assumed complete control, the Soviets were abolished, and a counter-revolutionary military dictatorship set up. The Bolshevik party was subjected to relentless persecution, especially its leader Lenin.

On July 5, 1917 Lenin went into hiding. This time it lasted for over a hundred trying days and nights. When it became too dangerous for him to remain in Petrograd, the Central Committee of the Party resolved to find its leader a less vulnerable hiding-place in the vicinity of Sestroretsk. There were many reliable people there, most of them workers of the local Arms Factory, who wholeheartedly supported the Bolshevik cause. Moreover, Sestroretsk was situated near the border with Finland. This was very important in case Lenin were forced by circumstances to flee the country at short notice. The protection of Lenin was entrusted to Nikolay Emelyanov, a worker of the Sestroretsk factory, an old hand in underground activities and a member of the Bolshevik Party since 1904. Emelyanov's house stood on the outskirts of Razliv, in a spot hidden from view by dense growths of lilac bushes and ash trees. Close by was a creek, linked with Lake Razliv by a narrow channel. Should an emergency arise, it would be possible to slip away unnoticed in a boat to the lake's opposite shore.

Accompanied by Emelyanov, Lenin arrived at the station of Razliv in the early morning hours of July 10. In a few minutes they were inside Emelyanov's outhouse. Lenin chose the hayloft for his quarters, as the safest place; bedding was laid out for him in the hay and a small table and chair installed.

The trying circumstances of the times notwithstanding, Lenin continued to direct the Party in its efforts to prepare the masses for socialist revolution. The Central Committee regularly supplied him with detailed information, most of the daily papers were delivered to him every day, and his colleagues from the Central Committee came over on a number of occasions to discuss vital political problems.

The shed where Lenin lived and worked for several days was transformed in 1925 into a memorial museum by a special decree of the Central Committee of the Party. On its façade a memorial plaque was put up bearing the following inscription: "Here, in the hayloft of this shed, Vladimir Ilyich Lenin, hiding from the persecution of the counter-revolutionary Provisional government, lived and worked for several days beginning with July 10 (23 O. S.), 1917." On the eve of Lenin's centenary a protective case of glass was put up over this historic monument to shelter it from the elements. Some of the household items used by Lenin during his stay here are on display in the shed, including a samovar and a copper kettle. Also extant is the kitchen range where Lenin's meals were cooked, and the ladder leading up to the hayloft.

Adjoining the shed is Emelyanov's house, a modest little structure. Close by is another house, once also the property of the Emelyanov family, which contains an exhibition of materials relating to this period of Lenin's life. This includes a photocopy of the manuscript of Lenin's *Political Situation*. Written by the leader on his first day at Razliv, these four theses contain a profound Marxist analysis of the political situation in the country after the events of July and define the tasks facing the Party in the circumstances then prevailing. Also on display are photocopies of Lenin's letters to the editors of the newspapers *New Life* and *The Proletarian Cause*, and a copy of his booklet *On Slogans* written in mid-July 1917. The booklet was published by the Kronstadt Committee of the Russian Social Democratic Workers' Party (Bolsheviks) for the 6th Congress of the Party.

Too long a sojourn at Razliv was fraught with danger, and a few days after his arrival there, late in the evening, Lenin was taken by Emelyanov across the lake to its opposite, uninhabited shore. The shed continued to serve as a link in the chain of contacts between Lenin and the Central Committee. Whenever a representative of the latter arrived, he would be ferried across the lake to Lenin. The opposite shore of Lake Razliv was a meadow where Emelyanov mowed his hay. He put up a hut of branches and twigs here and covered it with hay, and it was this hut that served as a dwelling for Lenin in the difficult summer of 1917. Vladimir Ilyich was described to the few people likely to wander into the area as a Finnish mower, supposedly hired for the season by Emelyanov. Emelyanov himself was also there — he did the mowing. With Lenin all the time, to act as a lookout, was Emelyanov's son Kolia. When the adults were at work, the boy kept watch, and made and tended a fire where they cooked their meals. In

Razliv

the thick underbrush close by a clearing was made, and two sections of tree-trunks brought over. One served as a table for Vladimir Ilyich, the other as a chair. He jokingly referred to the nook as his "green study".

In 1927, on the tenth anniversary of the October Revolution, the foundations of a memorial were laid at this very spot. Its unveiling took place on July 15, 1928. The author, Alexander Gegello, fashioned it in the strict and precise forms that alone could convey the greatness of the heroic epoch, the memories of which are associated with this plot of ground. Chiselled on the granite wall of the monument is the following inscription: "At this spot, where in July and August of 1917, in a hut built of branches, the leader of the World Revolution sheltered from the persecution of the bourgeoisie and wrote his book *The State and Revolution*, — here, in memory of those events, we have erected this hut of granite. The workers of the city of Lenin. 1927." Next to the monument stand a hut of poles and hay, and a haystack. These were originally put up under the supervision of Emelyanov. Nowadays they are renewed annually. Lenin's "hearth" and "green study" have been recreated a few steps away from the hut.

In 1964 a pavilion of granite, marble and glass, designed by Valentin Kirkhoglani, Norin, and Kondratyev, was erected a short distance away from the granite monument to house the museum. There is a memorial inscription on the outer wall, to the right of the doorway, which reads: "Here, on the shores of Lake Razliv, Vladimir Ilyich Lenin lived in hiding to escape arrest by the counter-revolutionary Provisional government. From here he continued to lead the Bolshevik Party, readying it for armed uprising." The exhibition opens with *Lenin in Razliv*, a sculpture by Venyamin Pinchuk, People's Artist of the USSR and State Prize laureate. On display in the pavilion are documents relating to Lenin's activities in Razliv, and a number of articles which help visualize Lenin's then surroundings. Also featured are photographs depicting the events of the summer of 1917, a map which shows Lenin's itinerary (worked out by himself) from Petrograd to Razliv, and, finally, the works he wrote in Razliv. Among these is the booklet *On Slogans*, whose theses contained the substance of the resolutions later adopted by the 6th Congress of the Party. In the booklet, as well as in other works written in Razliv, Lenin charted a new tactical course for the Bolshevik Party to follow at the new stage of the proletarian revolution that had set in. These works played an important role in preparing and carrying out the armed uprising of October 1917. There are a number of authentic newspapers on show, which carry articles written by Lenin. A prominent part of the display consists of documents relating to the Bolshevik Party's 6th Congress, which oriented the Party and the working class of Russia toward preparing for the armed uprising that was to come.

Razliv

The focal point of the exhibition is Lenin's masterpiece *The State and Revolution*. On display is an authentic copy of the first edition of the book, written in August and September 1917, photocopies of several of the manuscript sheets, and a replica of Lenin's well-known blue note-book entitled *Marxism and the State*, where he entered passages from Marx and Engels on questions relating to the state and the dictatorship of the proletariat. These entries were begun by Lenin during his emigré period in Switzerland, and he used the material in Razliv for his own book about the state. The section devoted to Lenin's *State and Revolution* also features excerpts from the current Programme of the CPSU which point the way to the development of the Soviet state and socialist democracy under present-day conditions.

Alongside the materials which illustrate Lenin's activities, the exhibition also features several objects which help visualize his way of life at that time. Displayed in show-cases are Lenin's *kosovorotka* (worker's shirt), a scythe, rake, kettle, and a mess-tin. These are duplicates of the articles actually used by Lenin (the originals are housed in the Central Lenin Museum in Moscow and in its Leningrad subsidiary). The boat which took Lenin across the lake to the hayfield is displayed against the background of a huge photorama of Lake Razliv.

In August 1917 the Central Committee of the Party arranged for Lenin to leave for Finland. He was provided with a false identity card and pass issued to one Konstantin Petrovich Ivanov, supposedly a worker of the Sestroretsk Arms Factory. The unique photograph of Lenin wearing a wig, specially taken for the pass, and copies of the pass itself and the identity card are on display. One late night in the beginning of August 1917 Lenin left the hut on the shore of Lake Razliv for good. His itinerary from Razliv to Finland is shown on a large map.

During the Great Patriotic War of 1941—45 the front line came to within a few kilometres of the Hut. At the foot of the monument Soviet soldiers swore loyalty to the Motherland, military units were presented with Guards' colours for outstanding achievement on the bat-tlefield, and soldiers and officers were decorated for bravery in action. At the turn-off point from the Maritime Highway to a four-kilometre-long road leading from Tarkhovka to the Hut stands the sculpture *Lenin in Razliv* by Pinchuk, and an unusual indicator consisting of a row of five twenty-metre-high piers, each carrying one letter to make up the word LENIN.

Like all the memorial places in any way linked with Lenin, the Shed and Hut museums are lovingly and painstakingly preserved. Both enjoy immense popularity. In the past three years alone they have seen about three million visitors from seventy-six countries.

Pavel Koloskov

1. The Hut: monument of granite: in the right foreground, replica of the hut and haystack

3. Lenin Memorial Museum: The Shed

4. The Shed with the hayloft window open, showing part of the interior

5. Lenin Memorial Museum: The Shed. Interior

6. View of Lake Razliv

7. View of the lake

8. The Hut: monument of granite

НА МЕСТЕ ГДЕ
В ИЮЛЕ И АВГУСТЕ
1917 ГОДА
В ШАЛАШЕ ИЗ ВЕТВЕЙ
СКРЫВАЛСЯ
ОТ ПРЕСЛЕДОВАНИЯ БУРЖУАЗИИ
ВОЖДЬ
МИРОВОГО ОКТЯБРЯ
И ПИСАЛ СВОЮ КНИГУ
„ГОСУДАРСТВО И РЕВОЛЮЦИЯ"
НА ПАМЯТЬ ОБ ЭТОМ
ПОСТАВИЛИ МЫ
ШАЛАШ ИЗ ГРАНИТА...
РАБОЧИЕ
ГОРОДА ЛЕНИНА
1927 г.

9. The Hut: monument of granite. Inscription on the monument

10. Replica of the hut and haystack

11. Lenin's "Green study"

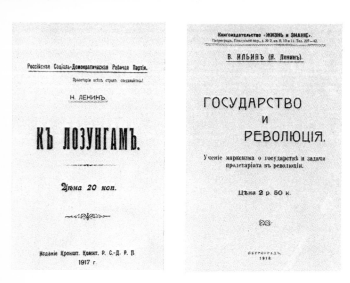

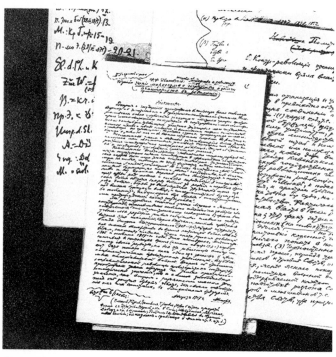

12. Booklets and manuscript articles by Lenin (photographs)

13. Lenin Memorial Museum: The Hut. Exhibition pavilion. *Lenin in Razliv* by V. Pinchuk

14. Lenin Memorial Museum: The Hut. General view of the exhibition pavilion

15. Lenin Memorial Museum: The Hut. Exhibition pavilion. Interior

16. Lenin Memorial Museum: The Hut. Exhibition pavilion. Entrance

17. Five piers erected at the turn-off point
from the Maritime Highway to a road
leading to the Lenin Memorial Museum, The Hut

PETRODVORETS

The parks, palaces and fountains of Peterhof, now Petrodvorets (since 1944), are a memorial — the only one of its kind — honouring Russia's triumph in her struggle for an outlet to the Baltic Sea in the first quarter of the eighteenth century. Its formal parks, its one hundred and forty-four fountains and three cascades, the gilded statues of the gods and heroes o-antiquity, the décor of the state rooms in its palaces — all these were meant to reify the conf cept of a victorious Russia "freely ranging the wide expanses of the seas", in the words of the poet Alexander Pushkin. Petrodvorets is a monument of immense artistic value. It is a gem in the treasure-house of art, one of the highest achievements of world culture, an embodiment of the creative genius and inspired toil of the Russian people.

The construction of Peterhof was begun in 1714. The site — hard by the very waters of the Gulf — was chosen by Peter the Great. He also outlined the main principles of layout for the central and eastern parts of the Lower Park, and conceived the idea of unifying the Great Palace, the Grotto, the Great Cascade and the Sea Canal into one compositional whole. The Tsar's expressed desire to make of Peterhof a residence "befitting the greatest monarchs of the age," plus a purely external resemblance between some of Peterhof's features and those of Versailles, led to the former being referred to as "the Russian Versailles". "It is often likened to Versailles," wrote the well-known Russian artist and art historian, Alexander Benois, "but that is a misunderstanding. Peterhof is absolutely unique, and its character is imparted to it by the sea. It is as though Peterhof were born of the foam of the sea, as though it were willed into being by the mighty king of the deep . . . The fountains in Peterhof are not an appendage to the ensemble, but its essence. They are a symbolic expression of the realm of water, a cloud of spray from that very sea which laps the shore at Peterhof." And that is true indeed — the dominant feature of the ensemble is its organic link with the sea, which the builders of Peterhof strove to attain at every stage of its construction.

Work on the initial project was conducted by Johann Braunstein, Jean-Baptiste Alexandre Le Blond, Niccolo Michetti, Mikhail Zemtsov, Piotr Eropkin, Timofey Usov, Grigory Ustinov, Isakov, the hydraulic engineer Vasily Tuvolkov and the fountain builder Paul Sualem, the sculptor Bartolommeo Carlo Rastrelli and his Russian assistants, and the master gardeners Leonardt van Harnigfelt and Anton Borisov. Each played a significant role in the work, displaying a fine artistic taste and an individual manner. An immensely important factor in the

Petrodvorets

creation of Peterhof were the construction teams of the "Chancellery of Works", the master gardeners and their assistants, fountain builders, painters, carvers, and other craftsmen, who were summoned from every corner of the country, or invited from abroad.

The Peterhof Palace and Park ensemble was, in the main, formed by 1723. Almost all the elements of the Lower Park and Upper Gardens' layouts had by that time taken shape, the Great and Monplaisir Palaces had been erected, and the water system feeding the fountains constructed. Peterhof's conduit system was built in 1720—21 to the design of the Russian hydraulic engineer Vasily Tuvolkov. This project called for the combined labour of over five thousand men every day. The total length of the conduit's canals is forty kilometres, and there are eighteen storage ponds situated at various points along the waterway, which can take in one million three hundred thousand cubic metres of water, and whose combined surface area is almost one hundred hectares. The Peterhof water-supply system is unique in that there are no water-towers or pumps whatsoever; it functions on the U-tube principle, the ponds and fountains being situated at different levels.

The entire royal residential complex — palaces, parks, and fountains — was officially opened on August 15, 1723. In the two centuries of its existence Peterhof grew into a vast palace and park complex widely known for its famous fountains, art collections, and festive illuminations. After the October Revolution of 1917 this imperial country residence became the property of its true owners — the people. All the palaces were transformed into museums immediately following the Revolution. The first party of workers who came to Peterhof on an excursion from Petrograd entered the halls of the Great Palace on May 18, 1918.

Much was done in the first ten post-revolutionary years (1918—27): an inventory was taken of all the museum treasures, new exhibitions were arranged, based on a scientific interpretation of the material. Ten Peterhof museums illustrated the course of Russian history and the development of her art and culture from the eighteenth to the early twentieth century.

If in 1918 the palaces and parks of Peterhof were visited by only seven thousand people, in 1938 the number of visitors reached two million. The peace of the country was, however, suddenly shattered by the treacherous onslaught of Nazi Germany. Work was immediately begun in Peterhof on saving and evacuating the art treasures concentrated here, in which museum staff and park workers alike took an active part. The sculptures were buried in the ground, other works of art were packed up and dispatched inland. In the three months that elapsed between the outbreak of war and the capture of Peterhof by the Nazis in September 1941, sixteen thousand museum exhibits were evacuated from the palaces and pavilions. The marbles and some of the bronze sculptures were hidden in secret caches in the territory of the Upper Gardens and Lower Park.

The Nazis set about the systematic destruction of Peterhof's cultural and artistic monuments. This was a premeditated barbarous act not warranted by military necessity. In the period between September 1941 and January 1944 the Hitlerites, engaging in outright plunder, took several thousand museum objects out of Peterhof. They destroyed the Great and Marly Palaces, the Olga and Rose Pavilions, the English Palace, ruthlessly demolished Monplaisir, the Hermitage Pavilion, the Tsarina's (Queen's) Pavilion and the Cottage, stole and shipped to Germany the remaining sculptures of the Great Cascade, including its central group of *Samson and the Lion,* cut down one third of the plantations — over twelve thousand trees. The damage inflicted by the Nazis on the Peterhof complex is estimated at fifty-six million roubles.

After the liberation of Peterhof in 1944, restoration of the palace and park complex, in accordance with a government decision, was promptly begun. Top priority was given to the Lower Park, and it was opened to visitors in July 1945. In August 1946 the first thirty-eight fountains were put into operation, the rest of the Great Cascade fountains, including its centrepiece *Samson Tearing Open the Jaws of the Lion,* were reactivated in September 1947. The missing bronze sculptures of the Great Cascade (*Samson, Volkhov, Neva* and the *Tritons*) were repeated by the Leningrad sculptors Vasily Simonov, Igor Krestovsky, Victor Ellonen and Nikolay Dydykin in 1946—56. Reconstructed in the postwar years were the Hermitage Pavilion, Peter the Great's Palace of Monplaisir, most of the interiors in the Great Palace, three cascades and a hundred and forty-four fountains. By 1968 the layout of the Upper Gardens had been recreated in its entirety, and the fountains and sculptures restored. The palace and park of Petrodvorets are today again one of the Soviet Union's most outstanding history and art museums.

The Petrodvorets ensemble includes two garden areas, — the Upper Gardens (15 hectares) and the Lower Park (102.5 hectares). The Upper Gardens are situated on the natural coastal terrace; the Lower Park, half a kilometre in width, stretches from the foot of the terrace down to the Gulf. The compositional link between the two areas is the Great Palace.

Petrodvorets

The author of the Palace's initial design is not known. The first variant of its layout was based on sketches made by Peter the Great himself, and work on its implementation was conducted from 1714 to 1716. Beginning with 1716 the project was headed by the gifted French architect Le Blond (1679—1719) who had been specially invited to Russia to supervise the construction of buildings in St Petersburg, the new capital. Le Blond emphasized the significance of the Palace as an official residence of the Tsar: he erected a columned vestibule, enlarged the doors and windows of the central hall and embellished it with panelling, painting, and carving. Death prevented Le Blond from completing the work, and in 1719 Johann Braunstein was appointed his successor. Braunstein made use of Le Blond's sketches and designs for the Palace's décor. The most significant job accomplished during this phase was the decoration of Peter's Study, for which fourteen carved oak panels were made to sketches by the French woodcarver and sculptor, Nicolas Pineau. From 1721 on the post of Architect-in-Chief was filled by Niccolo Michetti (?—1759), who added two side galleries to the edifice, terminating them in two-storey pavilions.

In 1745 work was begun on rebuilding the Palace, which was to last for several years. The whole project was designed and supervised by the outstanding Russian architect Francesco Bartolommeo Rastrelli (1700—1771). The new composition stemmed from the old concept: one central building adjoined by galleries, and two side pavilions. Rastrelli preserved the outward appearance of the structure, so typical of the architecture of the Petrine epoch, almost unchanged; enlarging the central part, he added two wings and joined them to the two side pavilions, the Palace Church and the Pavilion under Arms, by galleries. Inside the palace the architect designed a magnificent suite of state rooms and private chambers in the Baroque style. All the interiors were sumptuously decorated with gilded wood carvings, mirrors, ceiling paintings, and inlaid floors. Rastrelli had a number of talented painters working under him on the project: Ivan Vishniakov, the Belsky brothers, Bartolommeo Tarsia, Paolo Ballarini, Giuseppe Valeriani and Laurent Werner. The carved décor of the palace chambers was executed by unknown Russian craftsmen, the floors — by the parquet makers Zhdanov and Voronitsyn. In his interiors Rastrelli achieved exceptionally strong decorative effects. His State Staircase, Ballroom and Audience Room, which were still extant in 1941, were truly priceless monuments of mid-eighteenth century Russian art.

Petrodvorets

In the 1760s and 1770s some of the Great Palace's rooms were redone to conform with the newly emerged Classical style in architecture. The White Banquet Hall, the Throne and Chesme Rooms were redecorated, with white mouldings replacing the gilded wood carvings. The new ornamentation of these halls was designed by Yury Velten (1730—1801). Installed in the Chesme Room were twelve paintings by Jacob Philippe Hackaert, depicting various episodes of the victorious naval encounter in the Bay of Chesme during the Russo-Turkish War of 1768—74. Four other canvases on the same theme, all painted by Joseph Wright of Derby, hang in the Throne Room. Two Chinese Lobbies adorned with Chinese painting on lacquer were created to the design of Jean-Baptiste Vallin de la Mothe. In the middle of the nineteenth century the chambers of the Great Palace's eastern suite were redecorated to the designs, and under the supervision, of Andrey Stakenschneider (1802—1865).

Destroyed by the Nazi barbarians in the War of 1941—45, the Palace is now undergoing the long process of restoration under Vasily Savkov and Evgenia Kazanskaya. The work is being conducted by the Leningrad Construction Association "Restorer". In 1952—57 the recreation of the Palace's exterior was completed and the restoration of its interiors begun. Up to the present time the following chambers have been restored: the Picture Room, the White Banquet Hall, the Throne and Chesme Rooms, the Oak Study, the Chinese Lobbies, the Dressing Room, and the Partridge, Divan, and Crown Rooms.

The restorers have put in a tremendous amount of painstaking and complicated work in recreating the gilded carvings, the paintings, inlaid floors, stuccowork décor, and fireplaces. Once again the collection of three hundred and sixty-eight portraits by Pietro Rotari, the twelve-picture suite by Hackaert, and the canvases of Wright grace the palace's interiors. In the Throne Room the low relief panels of *The Return of Sviatoslav from the Danube* and *The Baptism of Olga*, executed in the 1770s by Mikhail Kozlovsky and Arkhip Ivanov, have been repeated, as were Ivan Prokofyev's allegoric low-relief medallions *Truth* and *Justice*. All the decorative finishing of the state rooms — the gilded carvings, the stucco mouldings, ceiling paintings, painted lacquer panels, and inlaid floors — has been recreated by Leningrad restorers.

The Great Palace is one of the most interesting and important museums in the country. Housed here are outstanding collections of both Russian and Western European painting, sculpture, and applied art (furniture, textiles, porcelains, etc.).

29

Petrodvorets

A magnificent view of the Great Cascade, the Sea Canal and the Gulf unfolds before the viewer from the paved terrace of the Great Palace. The Great Cascade, one of the most grandiose fountain complexes in the world, consists of sixty-four fountains and two hundred and fifty-five sculptures and decorative details. Speaking the language of allegory, the sculpture accomplishes the patriotic task of glorifying the Russian state. The centrepiece of the Cascade, and its largest fountain, *Samson Tearing Open the Jaws of the Lion* (height of jet 21 metres), is a monument honouring the Russians' victory over the Swedes at Poltava in June 1709. The statuary of the Great Cascade constitutes a priceless collection of works by the late eighteenth and early nineteenth century sculptors Ivan Martos, Feodosy Shchedrin, Fedot Shubin, Ivan Prokofyev, Jean-Dominique Rachette, and others. Part of the sculptures, the group of Samson among the others, were stolen by the Nazis during their occupation of the city, and the Grotto and the Cascades were blown up.

The Lower Park is divided into two parts, the eastern and the western, by the Sea Canal, which is lined on both sides by fountains, twenty-two in all. The Canal links the Great Palace and the Great Cascade with the Gulf. Situated in the eastern part of the park is the Chessboard Hill Cascade. The park's third cascade, the Golden Hill, is located in its western part, in a spot symmetrical to the site of Chessboard Hill. On the shore of the Gulf of Finland, at an equal distance from the Sea Canal, stand the Palace of Monplaisir and the Hermitage Pavilion, one in the eastern part of the park, the other in the western.

The Lower Park was a splendid example of the formal type of park. Its walks, alleys, palaces, pavilions and fountains are symmetrically disposed, and all the lawns, grass parterres, and reservoirs have regular geometric shapes. The formal character of the park was also emphasized by an abundance of topiary work (up to the 1790s), treillage screens lining the walks and parterres, and a wealth of statuary. The three radial alleys leading from the slope of the terrace to the Gulf, the Monplaisir Palace and the Hermitage Pavilion, are intersected by three other radial avenues which begin from the Marly Palace at the western extremity of the ensemble. The one in the middle, — the main avenue, — is known as the Marly Avenue and has a length of two kilometres. There are two fountains on the avenue — *Adam* in the eastern and *Eve* in the western parts of the park. The eight alleys which lead from each of these fountains to different parts of the park form two *étoiles* (star-shaped designs characteristic of the formal park).

Petrodvorets

Situated in the eastern area of the park is the Palace of Monplaisir, a unique monument of early eighteenth century Russian architecture and artistic culture. Among those who took part in the building and decoration of Monplaisir (1714—22) were the architects Braunstein, Le Blond, Michetti, the painters Philippe Pillement, Fiodor Vorobyov, and Stepan Bushuyev. All the façades of the Palace are decorated in a simple and laconic manner, and this is contrasted by the sumptuousness of its interior décor, which unites in a harmonious combination ceiling paintings, lacquered panels, Dutch tiles and elegant stuccowork mouldings. Monplaisir houses an extensive collection of seventeenth and early eighteenth century Dutch, Italian, and Flemish paintings, forming the first picture gallery in Russia.

The Palace of Monplaisir, one of the most "revered relics of Russian history," in the words of Belinsky (the outstanding Russian literary critic), was turned by the Nazis into a barracks and a strongpoint, and suffered serious damage. Today it is completely restored. New panels for its Lacquer Room were executed by Palekh artists working under Nikolay Zinovyev, People's Artist of the USSR. The main decorative element of the Palace's galleries are pictures by seventeenth and eighteenth century Dutch, Flemish, and Italian masters. Of particular interest in the Central Hall of Monplaisir are the ceiling painting and stucco mouldings which depict, respectively, personages of the Italian *commedia dell'arte*, and allegories of the seasons and the four elements. The Central Hall is adjoined by the Lacquer Room, the Kitchen, and the Pantry. The Kitchen houses a collection of copper kitchenware of the early eighteenth century, tin plates produced in England and hallmarked by the foremost craftsmen of the time, and Delft faience. In the pantry is a collection of artistic glass made by Russian masters in the first quarter of the eighteenth century. Three other chambers adjoin the Central Hall from the west: the Sea Room, whose windows look out on the Gulf of Finland and whose walls are adorned in the lower part with tiles depicting the thirteen types of sailing ships used by the Russian navy in the eighteenth century; the Bedroom, where Peter's personal effects are on display, and the Secretary's Room.

The Monplaisir Palace is fronted by a garden with figured flowerbeds and fountains. A straight avenue connects the Monplaisir ensemble with Chessboard Hill. Also situated in the eastern part of the park are the trick fountains: *Benches*, *Little Oak*, and *Umbrella*; a singular aquatic obelisk named the *Pyramid* Fountain, and the mechanical fountain *The Sun*.

Petrodvorets

Located symmetrically to Monplaisir in the western half of the park, on the shoreline of the Gulf, is the Hermitage Pavilion. It rests on a brick stylobate, and is surrounded by a moat. The Pavilion was erected in 1722—25 under the supervision of Braunstein. One of the most perfect Russian architectural monuments of the first quarter of the eighteenth century, the Hermitage stands out for the lightness and elegance of its faultless proportions and for the beauty of its architectural forms. A splendid panorama of the Gulf of Finland and Kronstadt unfolds from the windows of the Central Hall on the first floor. The Hall itself is adorned with canvases by seventeenth and eighteenth century Western European artists. Ruined by the Nazis during the war, the Hermitage pavilion was rebuilt and opened to visitors in 1952.

The Marly Palace, also in the Park's western area, was designed and built by Braunstein almost simultaneously with the Hermitage. It is sited on the bank of a rectangular pond and is the centre of an ensemble which includes the Golden Hill Cascade, a group of fountains and an orchard. During the war the Nazis blew up the Marly Palace with a delayed-action mine. The façades of the palace were reconstructed in 1954—55. The restoration of its interiors and, for that matter, of the entire western area of the Lower Park, is currently in progress.

A city of palaces, parks and fountains, Petrodvorets enjoys world renown. Each year over two and a half million people come to admire the monuments of Russian culture and art concentrated here, to take in the extraordinary charm and inimitable beauty of Petrodvorets and breathe its invigorating, crisp sea air, to walk its shaded alleys, and listen to the murmur of its age-old trees and the symphony of its fairyland fountains.

The resurrected palace and park ensemble of Petrodvorets has today acquired an added significance: it serves not only as a monument of the history and art of the past, but symbolizes, moreover, the inspired toil and creative genius of the Soviet People.

Ilya Gurevich

18. View of the Great Palace and the Great Cascade

20. The Great Cascade. The Samson Fountain

21. The Great Cascade. The Western Cascade Stairway

22. The Great Cascade. *Galatea*, decorative sculpture by Jean-Dominique Rachette

25. The Upper Gardens. The Oak Fountain

26. The Upper Gardens. The Pavilion under Arms

27. The Great Cascade
on a festive night

28. The Upper Gardens. A fountain of the Square Pond

29. The Upper Gardens. The Neptune Fountain

30. The Great Palace. The Portrait Room

31. The Throne Room

33. The West Chinese Lobby

34. The Lower Park. The Marly Palace. View across the Marly Pool

35. The Lower Park. The Triton Cloche Fountain

36. The Lower Park. The Hermitage Pavilion

37. The Lower Park. The Hermitage Pavilion. View of the hall on the first floor

38. The Lower Park. View of the Monplaisir Garden with the Sheaf Fountain

39. The Lower Park. Sea Terrace before the Monplaisir Palace

40. The Lower Park. The Monplaisir Palace. Gallery

41. The Lacquer Room

42. The Sea Room

43. The Central Hall

44. The Lower Park.
The Roman Fountains

45. The Lower Park. The Nymph Fountain; the Whale Fountain

46. The Lower Park. The Adam Fountain. Sculpture by Giovanni Bonazza

47. The Lower Park. View of the flower parterres before the Chessboard Hill Cascade

48. The Lower Park. Figures of dragons at the top of the Chessboard Hill Cascade

49. The Lower Park. *Psyche*, 19th-century copy of a sculpture by Antonio Canova

50. The Lower Park. The Pyramid Fountain

PUSHKIN

Many books have been written about the palaces and parks of the town of Pushkin, formerly Tsarskoye Selo. The beauty of these remarkable creations of architecture and park design has been sung by poets, painters and graphic artists alike. They are the subject of some of Alexander Pushkin's most inspired verse. The name of the great Russian poet who came here in 1811 as a twelve-year-old youngster to study at the Lyceum has become forever a part of the city's heritage: in 1937, on the centenary of the poet's death, Tsarskoye Selo, by government decree, was given the name of Pushkin.

The main landmark of Tsarskoye Selo, founded in 1710 as a country residence for Catherine I, the wife of Peter the Great, is the Catherine, or Great Palace and the three hundred hectares of parks which surround it. The creation of this ensemble, which embodies the achievements of the Russian artistic culture of its time, was started in the 1740s—1750s.

The Palace, begun in 1744 by Alexey Kvasov and Savva Chevakinsky on the former site of an original mansion of modest size, was brought to completion by Francesco Bartolommeo Rastrelli in 1756. Its three hundred and six metre long façade is the compositional axis of the ensemble. Even today the Palace grips the imagination with the enormity of its proportions and the sumptuousness of its décor. Numberless columns, pilasters, moulded ornaments and sculptured figures lend an air of sublime elegance and festive radiance to the structure. The exquisite contrast between the azure of the walls, the white of the columns, and the gold of the balconies' openwork grilles is a veritable feast for the eye. Designed in the magnificent Baroque style, the palace formed a suitable setting for the ceremonial life of the imperial court.

The state rooms of the Palace are adorned with gilded wood carvings, stuccowork décor, precious silks, objects in stone, and inlaid floors of valuable species of wood. The fine examples of Russian and foreign arts and crafts, assembled here — the seventeenth and eighteenth century paintings, the Chinese *objets d'art*, the bronzes, porcelains, glass, decorative textiles, and furniture — form valuable museum collections.

Pushkin

Soon after the outbreak of the War of 1941—45 all the archives and part of the collections were evacuated inland. The halls of the Palace were wrecked by the Nazis, and are today being restored as a museum of Russian eighteenth and nineteenth century architecture and interior decoration. The author of the overall project for the restoration of the Catherine Palace and Park complex is Kedrinsky. Work has been completed on the Picture Hall and the Dining Room for Courtiers in Attendance, both of Rastrelli's creation; the restoration of Rastrelli's Golden Suite and the Throne Room is under way; of the seventeen interiors so far restored some have a décor in the refined Classicist style of Cameron, the others represent the majestic severity of Stasov's Empire décor.

The visitor can learn about the Palace's history, the original aspect of its interiors, and the methods used in its restoration from an exhibition now open to the public. This occupies several rooms, repaired but not as yet restored. One of these rooms houses materials illustrating the history of the famous Amber Room, and a collection of objects in amber (mosaic caskets, snuff-boxes, checkers, chesspieces and various knick-knacks), which serve to display the decorative potentialities of the material. The only reminder of the ineffable beauty of this room in the past is a painting in oils, executed by Alexey Bobylev, and some documentary photographs, taken before the war.

The Amber Room was once decorated with fifty-five panels composed of pieces of polished amber. The panels were executed in 1709 from the designs of Andreas Schlüter, and presented to Peter the Great in 1716 as a diplomatic gift by Friedrich Wilhelm of Prussia. In 1755 Rastrelli used them to line the walls in one of the chambers of the state suite, supplementing the panels with a décor of gilt carved wood, twenty-four mirror pilasters, and agate and jasper mosaic pictures. The striking combination of the resplendent Baroque forms of the carvings and pilasters with the exquisite patterns created by the varicoloured pieces of amber was, from the point of view of decorative effect, a stroke of genius.

Pushkin

The Amber Room, that brilliant and sole example of the use of amber in wall décor, remained the pride of the Catherine Palace for almost two hundred years. During the War of 1941—45 the Nazis stole the amber panels and shipped them to Königsberg (now Kaliningrad). When the advancing Soviet Army neared the city in 1945 the Germans hid the stolen art treasures. All attempts to recover the amber panels have so far proved unsuccessful.

Situated next to the Amber Room is the Picture Hall, the largest chamber in the northern part of the palace. Its décor consists of canvases by Western European artists of the seventeenth and the first quarter of the eighteenth centuries. Quite a few of the one hundred and thirty Italian, French, Netherlandish, Flemish, German and Austrian paintings housed here are works of very high artistic merit: landscapes by Jan Both, architectural landscapes by Emmanuel de Witte, genre scenes by Adriaen van Ostade and David Teniers, mythological scenes by Jacques Blanchard and Luca Giordano, the allegories of sculpture and music by Jean-Marc Nattier, and others. Among the most interesting are two pairs of companion paintings — battle scenes by the French artists Jacques Courtois and Pierre Denis Martin the Younger. The latter's works depict the battle of Poltava, fought on June 27, 1709, and that of Lesnaya, which took place on September 28, 1708, both Russian victories in the Great Northern War. The pictures, which completely cover the walls, are symmetrically arranged according to size, shape, and colour so as to produce a pleasing overall pattern. This type of hanging was typical of all eighteenth century palace picture galleries.

The Picture Hall could never have been restored if almost the entire collection of paintings had not been evacuated inland at the start of the war. Also restored are the Hall's tall stoves lined with painted Dutch tiles, most of them authentic. The carved Baroque door surrounds, their gilding all aglow in the light, were wrought by the woodcarver Alexey Kochuyev and other craftsmen. The new ceiling painting, executed by Yakov Kazakov and his assistants, is a copy of the ceiling over the Main Staircase of the Winter Palace in Leningrad. The Picture

Hall, like the restored Dining Room for Courtiers in Attendance, and the Grand Hall, now in the process of restoration, is illustrative of the Baroque masters' ability to create a single harmonious ensemble out of an extremely wide range of decorative elements.

The walls of the Dining Room are adorned with carved floral garlands and rocailles, all beautifully reflected in symmetrically placed mirrors. The furniture was executed to sketches by Rastrelli and includes a set of gilded arm-chairs and a table. The Hunter's Service, displayed on the table, was made in the 1760s at the Imperial Porcelain Factory, the first in Russia.

In the last third of the eighteenth century Russian architecture came to be dominated by Classicism, a style which replaced the Baroque. During this period some of Rastrelli's halls were redecorated by Charles Cameron (1740—1812), an architect and classical scholar, who came to work in Russia in 1779. Cameron based the décor of the Green Dining Room, for example, on motifs of antique art. The pale-green walls with reliefs in white — ivy garlands, vases, and figures of maidens and youths, borrowed from antique paintings which adorned a Pompeian villa — are enlivened by the tender pink backgrounds of the medallions with dancing cupids, and by several low reliefs of mythological subjects, executed by Martos. The white-and-green chairs, and the bronze fire-irons and fire-guards were made for this hall from drawings by Cameron. All the rooms in the northern part of the Palace, whose interiors were designed by Cameron, have been completely restored: the Blue and the Chinese Drawing Rooms, the Painting and Sculpture Lobbies, and others.

The Marble Study of Alexander I and the adjoining Vaulted Passage and Oval Anteroom have been restored after drawings by Vasily Stasov, a nineteenth century architect. The walls of these rooms are lined with warm-toned artificial marble, — rose in the Study, and ivory-tinted in the other two interiors, — and the ceilings are ornamented with painting. The walnut furniture of strict Empire forms was executed from Stasov's sketches. All tours of the Palace's interiors end in the Church Antechamber, designed by Stasov. The gleaming gold framings of the wall panels and plafonds, and the gold of the capitals, bases and the standard lamps, stand out beautifully against the spotless white of the walls and columns. The hall is today used for poetry and music recitals.

The eastern and western façades of the Palace overlook the oldest parts of the Catherine and Alexander Parks. The avenue traversing the two parks lies on the main axis of the complex, which passes through the centre of the Palace, and about which the various elements of the layout are symmetrically disposed. The parks were conceived as an extension, as it were, of the palace halls, their walks were reminiscent of green corridors, and their vegetation was clipped to resemble green walls, vaulted passages, and niches.

The regular part of the Catherine or Old Garden, forty-two hectares in area, which stretches before the Palace's eastern façade, has preserved its eighteenth century layout. The terraces, divided into two symmetrical parts by the main avenue, rise all the way to the Palace. Situated on the uppermost terrace but one are embroidery parterres with patterns of fragmented brick and coal on pinkish yellow sand, repeating, as it were, the intricate ornamental designs of the Palace's parquet floors. Flanking the parterres are rectangular plantations of tall trees surrounded by hedges of low clipped limes. There are similar enclosures on the next terrace lower down. The lime hedges were planted in the 1960s, and when they reach the height of four to five metres, topiary gardeners will trim them down into green "walls". At the foot of the rise, below the terraces, stretches the formal Lower Garden, recreated after old drawings and plans. The restoration of the park which was seriously damaged in the war is being conducted in accordance with extant eighteenth century materials; the author of the project is Natalya Tumanova. Work on the terraces in front of the Palace has been completed; the pools on the lowermost terrace have been restored to their former shapes, which repeat those of the Palace's Baroque mirrors. The five hundred metre long Hermitage Avenue, which starts from the Palace's main entrance and leads down to the Hermitage, is graced with marble sculptures by eighteenth century Italian masters of the Venetian school — Pietro Baratta, Antonio Tarsia, and Giovanni Zorzoni. The stylistic unity of the regular park is further accentuated by two pavilions in the Baroque style — the Hermitage and the Grotto. As Rastrelli saw it, the sculptural décor and the vivid combination of azure and white on the façades of these little palaces which terminate the vistas of the two intersecting axial avenues, serve to blend them into one harmonious and triumphant accord with the Catherine Palace.

In the 1770s a landscape park, designed by Vasily Neyelov and Charles Cameron, was laid out south of the regular park. It is a sizable piece of land — sixty hectares of gently undulating ground — with spacious meadows, artificial pools, and picturesque groves and clumps of trees. There are over thirty decorative structures by outstanding masters in this landscape park, the first of its kind in the country. One of the distinctive features of the Catherine Park is the presence here of monuments glorifying Russian arms. Erected in the 1770s were the Kagul obelisk, the Morea Column, and the Chesme Column, all dedicated to the victories won by Russian forces in the Russo-Turkish War of 1768—74 (designed by Antonio Rinaldi and Vasily Neyelov). The practice of erecting monuments to commemorate military victories was customary in ancient Rome. It was revived by Catherine II in her park here and subsequently became a widespread tradition in Russia.

Cameron created an inimitable architectural ensemble of the classic type on the border between the formal and the landscaped parts of the Park. This consisted of the Cameron Gallery, named in his honour and intended to serve as a promenade walk, the Cold Baths with the Agate Rooms, and the Hanging Garden which links the ensemble to the Catherine Palace. Taken together, these structures foimed a sort of modern version of a classic theme — the thermae of ancient Rome. Another passionate admirer of antique art was the Italian Giacomo Quarenghi (1744—1817). The author of such major edifices as the Academy of Sciences, the Smolny Institute and the Currency Bank in St Petersburg, Quarenghi began his Russian career in Tsarskoye

Selo in the 1780s, designing several park pavilions, among them Concert Hall and the romantic Kitchen "Ruins" — a small brick building with genuine antique columns and a frieze — which, with their simple yet harmonious forms, epitomize the spirit of Classicism. They merge perfectly with their natural setting, — a result of the joint efforts of the architect Cameron and the gardener Joseph Busch. Quarenghi's finest creation in Tsarskoye Selo is the Alexander Palace, which he built in the 1790s.

Reflected in the smooth waters of the Big Lake in the centre of the Catherine Park are the classically strict contours of the Marble Bridge, built of Ural marble to the design of Neyelov. The Park is also adorned with a variety of decorative structures: ancient ruins, Chinese arbours, and buildings in a stylized medieval Gothic.

The Catherine Park was in the main brought to completion towards the end of the eighteenth century. All later alterations in, and additions to, the ensemble had for the most part to do with the Catherine Palace. During the first quarter of the nineteenth century construction work in the palace and park was conducted by Vasily Stasov. Built in this period were the monumental cast-iron gate in memory of the War of 1812, designed by Stasov, the *Milkmaid* Fountain with the figure of a girl executed by Pavel Sokolov, and the imposing granite terrace, the work of Luigi Rusca. In the 1820s the Alexander Park also acquired a new romantic look. Numerous monuments in the pseudo-Gothic style were designed and erected here by Adam Menelas — the White Tower, the Arsenal, the Chapelle Tower, and others. Today the Alexander Park serves as a recreation zone for the residents of Leningrad. The territory of the Catherine Park has been made a museum zone.

Galina Khodasevich

51. Monument to Alexander Pushkin in the Lyceum Garden

53. The Catherine Palace. The garden front

52. View of the Lyceum from the entrance to Alexander Park

54. Parterre in front of the Catherine Palace

55. The Catherine Palace. The State Staircase

56. The Dining Room for Courtiers in Attendance

57. The Bedroom

58. The Green Dining Room

59. The Chinese Drawing Room

60. The Blue Drawing Room

61. The Picture Hall

62. The Agate Rooms. View of the pavilion from the Catherine Park

63. The Agate Room

64. The Cameron Gallery. View of the southern colonnade

66. The Catherine Park. The Big Lake with the Chesme Column

65. The Catherine Park. The Mirror Pools and the Upper Baths Pavilion

67. The Catherine Park. The Turkish Bath

68. The Catherine Park. The Admiralty Pavilion

69. The Catherine Park. The Grotto Pavilion

70. View in the Catherine Park with the Evening Hall Pavilion

71. The Catherine Park. The Milkmaid Fountain. Sculpture by Pavel Sokolov

72. The Catherine Park. Bridge near the Squeaking Summerhouse

73. The Catherine Park. The Squeaking Summerhouse

74. View of a larch walk in the Catherine Park

75. View in the Catherine Park in winter, with the Concert Hall

76. The Grand Caprice linking the Alexander Park with the Catherine Park

77. Summerhouse of the Grand Caprice

78. The Alexander Park. The Chapelle Tower in winter

79. A walk in the Alexander Park

80. The Alexander Park. The Chinese Bridge

LOMONOSOV

The palaces and parks of Lomonosov* (formerly Oranienbaum) form a complex whose component parts were created in the course of the eighteenth century. Its beginnings were laid with the erection, in 1710—25, of the Great Palace and the creation of the Lower Garden by the architects Mario Giovanni Fontana (active in the first half of the eighteenth century) and Johann Gottfried Schadel (1680—1752) for Alexander Menshikov, a close associate of Peter the Great. The skillfully achieved compositional unity of the palace and the park spoke of a fine feeling for the synthesis of architecture and nature. Making the most of the relief of the terrain, the architects placed the palace on the top of the natural coastal terrace, with its main, northern façade facing the Gulf. A regular garden, with trimmed trees and shrub hedges and a geometric pattern of walks and parterres, was laid out before the palace. The park and the palace are connected by a system of terraces and staircases which lend the structure a dignified and monumental look. None of the many successive lords of the palace was particularly interested in preserving the layout and decorative finish of this eighteenth century architectural monument. Only the outside of the building has retained, in the main, its initial aspect, which makes the palace into a rare monument of the Petrine epoch.

In the 1750s to 1770s Oranienbaum was once again the scene of large-scale construction work. This involved the creation of a new spacious park, named the Upper, and the erection on its territory of new palaces and pavilions by Antonio Rinaldi (c. 1710—1794). Rinaldi, who spent most of his creative life in Russia, belonged to that generation of architects whose careers encompassed both the dominance of the Baroque in Russian art and the emergence and consolidation in it of the new style of Classicism. That is why Rinaldi's creations are a living record of the changes which Russian architecture was undergoing in those years. After the Baroque masterpieces of his Oranienbaum period, Rinaldi was to design such Classicist buildings as the palace at Gatchina and the Marble Palace in St Petersburg.

---

* The city was named Lomonosov in 1948 in honour of the Russian scientist Mikhail Lomonosov, who founded a factory of stained-glass artware and mosaic smalts in the village of Ust-Ruditsa near Oranienbaum.

Lomonosov

Rinaldi's first project in Oranienbaum, the Palace of Peter III (built 1758—62), was initially one of a group of structures which made up the "play fortress" of Peterstadt, where the heir to the Russian throne, and later Emperor (since 1762), though long past childhood, was fond of staging military games. It is difficult to visualize today that this was once the site of an arsenal, a guardhouse, and a large number of wooden outbuildings. The fortress was built to comply with all the precepts of the science of fortification, i. e. with ramparts, moat, drawbridges and all. Rinaldi imparted an air of severity and monumentality to the palace, which one usually associates with a fortified structure, yet the décor of its façades is not devoid of that refinement which is so typical of mid-eighteenth century pleasure pavilions. The general impression of lightness and elegance is enhanced by the openwork grilles which adorn the balconies and the French windows of the top floor. The interiors of the palace's ground floor are undecorated — in the eighteenth century they all served as utility rooms. Today they house an exhibition of materials — plans, designs, and drawings — devoted to the history of the Lomonosov palace and park ensemble. The six rooms of the top floor are ornamented with stuccowork, painted lacquers, carving, pictures, and silks.

The principal chamber of the palace is the Picture Hall. Its décor consists of paintings, entirely covering the walls so as to merge into an overall decorative pattern. There are sixty-three canvases all told, each outlined by a silvered fillet and divided from the others only by a narrow strip of black framing. The visual effect is much like that produced by a large and colourful tapestry with its strong play of light and shade. The pictures themselves belong to many Western European schools of the seventeenth and eighteenth centuries. A distinguishing feature of the décor in the Hall, the Study and the Bedroom is the unique lacquer painting on the doors, the panels in the lower part of the walls, and the door and window reveals. It was executed by a gifted serf artist, Fiodor Vlasov, in the Rococo style characterized by the use of Chinoiserie motifs. The Palace's interiors retain exquisite stuccowork décor on the ceilings. The most interesting is that of the Boudoir, with views of Peterstadt, sailing boats on the Lower Pond, galloping soldiers, and trophies of arms all executed in low relief on the coving.

Lomonosov

In the nineteenth century the grounds of the palace were incorporated into the Upper Park. This, the eastern part of the park, is one of the most picturesque in the complex. The western part of the Upper Park with its Chinese Palace, Coasting Hill Pavilion and other structures was known in the eighteenth century as "Her Majesty's (Catherine II's) Own *Dacha*" (country estate). This spacious area was designed by Rinaldi. It is a very interesting artistic achievement in that it combines two principal types of garden architecture — the formal garden and the landscape park. The section of the Chinese Palace, stretching as far as the Coasting Hill Pavilion, has a regular layout. Traces of the former regular planning remain in the axial and radial layout of the walks, the rectangul aropenings at the intersections, and the parterres of the Chinese Palace. In front of the palace's southern façade are two marble statues, *Apollo Belvedere* and *Artemis with a Doe* (eighteenth century copies of antique originals), and two bronze statues, *Apollo* and *Venus de' Medici* (nineteenth century casts from old models). The northern façade is fronted by marble sculptures wrought by unknown eighteenth century masters. The landscape park lies west of the Coasting Hill Pavilion. Winding pathways, picturesque clumps of freely growing trees, figured ponds composing a singular aquatic labyrinth — all these lend the landscape an inimitable charm. Skillfully realizing the potentialities inherent in the scenery of northern Russia, the architect created here a truly beautiful landscape park.

The ensemble of Her Majesty's private estate served as the Empress's summer pleasure grounds Architecturally and artistically the two main structures of the ensemble — the Chinese Palace and the Coasting Hill Pavilion — were solved in the Rococo style. Rinaldi's Oranienbaum palaces are the only monuments of this architectural style in Russia.

The name "Chinese Palace" stems from the Chinoiserie décor in three of its interiors, and the wealth of Chinese and Japanese art objects which grace many of its rooms. It is one of those singular structures which combine the specific features of a palace with those of a garden pavilion. The one-storey building (the second storey on the south side was added in the 1850s by Andrey Stakenschneider) on a low paved platform enclosed by a light openwork grille is of elongated proportions. The projecting central part of its northern façade is adorned by columns and pilasters, over which are a pediment and a shell and garlands motif. The restrained architecture of the Palace's façades stands in deliberate contrast to the extraordinary wealth and variety of the decorative finish of its interiors. Alexander Benois, the famous Russian art historian, characterized this architectural masterpiece in the following words: "The Chinese Palace in Oranienbaum is one of the most remarkable monuments of the eighteenth century for the stylistic unity and elegance of its artistic finish ... The painted decorations, stucco mouldings, pictures and architectural details all merge into one integral whole which in its purely musical effect evokes associations with the sonatas of Haydn and Mozart."

The palace took six years to complete (1762—68). Many skillful craftsmen participated in its building and decoration, and it is due to their talents that the complicated architectural and ornamentational problems which arose in the process of construction were brilliantly resolved. Built in three suites, the palace has the form of the Russian letter П. The seventeen interiors that have come down to our day are outstanding for the superb taste and refined elegance of their décor.

The northern suite — that of the state chambers — begins with the Hall of the Muses, which is adorned with painting and gilded mouldings. The plafond *The Triumph of Venus*, and the painting on the walls and coving were executed by the Italian artist Stefano Torelli. Depicted on the wall panels are the nine Muses, goddesses of the arts, and cupids playfully impersonating the gods are represented on the coving. The Buglework Room was so named because its walls are adorned with buglework panels. They were made in France in the workshop of de Chéne. Twelve panels, hand embroidered in chenille on a silvery iridescent buglework background, and depicting exotic landscapes with birds, are enclosed in carved gilt frames. The latter were executed by highly-skilled Russian craftsmen. Situated in the centre of the palace is the Grand Hall, whose décor consists of coloured stucco, painting, gilded mouldings, and mosaics. Over the doors are two medallion portraits in low relief, one representing Peter the Great and the other, his daughter Elizabeth. Both are the work of Anne-Marie Collot, a pupil of Etienne-Maurice Falconet, the author of the *Bronze Horseman*.

Lomonosov

The suite of state rooms includes the Hall of the Muses, the Blue Parlour, the Buglework Room, the Grand Hall, the Lilac Drawing Room, the Small and the Large Chinese Rooms. Both ends of this range of rooms are joined at right angles to two lesser suites. Of these, the eastern used to belong to Grand Prince Paul, son of Catherine II, and consists of the Pink Parlour, the Damask Bedroom, the Boudoir, and Paul's Study. The other, the western, once occupied by the Empress herself, includes the Chinese Bedroom, the Dressing Room, the Portrait Room, and Catherine II's Study. The eastern suite is linked to the Grand Hall by way of the Anteroom and the Wardrobe Room.

The dominant element in the décor of the interiors is painting. It was executed by Italian masters of the Venetian Academic school — Giovanni-Battista Pittoni, Gasparo Diziani, Jacopo Guarana, Francesco Zugno, Domenico Maggiotto, Francesco Zuccarelli. Significant, too, is the role played by the stuccowork ornamentation of the walls and coving. The muted colours of the walls combine excellently with the gilding to create a strong decorative effect. The unique parquetry of the interiors is also an integral part of the décor. The crafting of these floors involved such techniques as inlay, incrustation, carving and pokerwork. The surface layer of each floor is pieced together of thin plates of local (maple, birch, pear, apple and oak) and foreign (mahogany, rosewood, lemon, larch, amaranth, Persian walnut, sandalwood, ebony, and boxwood) species of wood. The beautiful patterns of the floors echo the decorative design of the corresponding ceiling.

The Palace houses a rare collection of eighteenth century applied art: Russian and Meissen porcelains, Oriental lacquers and enamels. The stools, settees, and console tables were carved and gilded by Russian craftsmen to sketches by Rinaldi; the marquetry furniture — the bureaux, commodes and tables — was brought from France, Germany, and England. Works of Russian and Western European art mingle very well in the interior décor of the palace.

Situated in the western part of the park is the Coasting Hill Pavilion, designed by Rinaldi. This is a rare phenomenon in the Russian architecture of the second half of the eighteenth century. The foundations of the Pavilion were laid in 1757, but the construction and décor were carried out later, between 1762 and 1774. The Coasting Hill was an amusement complex consisting of a pavilion and a long roadway resting on trestlework, with four ups and downs ("hills"), the whole surrounded by a columned gallery whose flat roof served as a promenade. The coasting, though suggested by tobogganing, a favourite Russian winter pastime, was a summer amusement. The little cars used for the purpose did in fact resemble pretty decorated sledges, but they ran on wheels for which special grooves had been made in the roadway. These cars were constructed by the inventor Andrey Nartov, who also devised a method for returning them to the starting point; Nartov's principle was used in all subsequent structures of this type. In the nineteenth century the trestle fell into decay and was dismantled.

The top floor of the pavilion is taken up by the Round Hall and the adjoining Porcelain and White Rooms. It is reached by an inner staircase leading from a small first-floor vestibule to the Upper Landing. The interiors of the Vestibule, the Staircase and the Landing are embellished with white stucco mouldings of stylized shells, floral wreaths, garlands, branches, and flowers. The ground colour is pale blue or pale green, which agree very well with the refined, delicate colour schemes of the Pavilion's interiors.

The decorative finish of the Round Hall, which is the compositional centre of the upper floor, is a masterpiece for its harmonious blend of painting, gilded mouldings, and coloured artificial marbles. The walls and the low dome, with its painted *trompe-l'œil* treillage roof showing a piece of sky, were executed in 1767—68 by the Italian artist Serafino Barozzi; the gilded mouldings were wrought by Giani and Russian craftsmen in 1766—67. Stefano Torelli's overdoors with *Neptune*, *Naiad and a Dolphin*, and *Amphitrite*, done specially for this hall in 1768, are examples of decorative painting at its very best. The floor, with its exquisite patterns of variously coloured artificial marbles, is an extremely rare sample of eighteenth century decorative techniques. The wealth of ornamental possibilities inherent in marble allowed it to be used for lining the fireplaces and door jambs. All work in artificial marble was done in 1767 by Spinelli, an Italian, jointly with Russian masters. In 1952—58 the interior décor of the Round Hall was reproduced by the Special Restoration Workshops of Leningrad.

Lomonosov

The Porcelain Room derives its name from its decorative furnishings. These consist of about thirty porcelain sculptures specially ordered from the Meissen factory and executed there in 1772—74 by Johann Joachim Kaendler and Victor Acier. The groups *The Triumph of Amphitrite*, *Neptune and Thetis*, and *Victoria* are allegories honouring the Russian Navy's victory in the battle of Chesme in 1770. The other pieces are symbolic of trade and the various arts. The porcelains are arranged on shelves with underprops shaped as heads of cupids or figures of monkeys and eaglets, executed in high relief, with details in the round.

The White Room is adorned with white panels featuring stuccowork ornaments in the shape of stylized branches and shells, and trophies of arms. These accord well with the pale greenish ground colour of the walls and with the palest lilac, green, and cream tints of the floor.

The palaces and parks of Oranienbaum served as the summer residences of the royal family and the nobility up to 1917. In August 1918 they were nationalized and declared the property of the people. In 1922 the ensemble was converted into a museum zone. In the very first months of the War of 1941—45 the art collections housed in these museums were evacuated inland. Oranienbaum was soon cut off by Nazi troops, but managed to hold out against fierce enemy attacks. It became an isolated stronghold in the defence perimeter of Leningrad; from here an offensive was launched in January 1944 which played an important role in lifting the siege of Leningrad. The architectural monuments of Oranienbaum, generally speaking, survived the war, although the parks and many of the buildings suffered serious damage. Steps were taken in 1945—46 to remedy the destruction caused and restoration work was begun.

The popularity of Lomonosov's museums tends to grow from year to year. In 1964, 166,500 visitors were recorded, whereas the attendance figure for the 1974 season rose to 255,000. Dedicated to the goal of building a new culture based on Communist principles, the Soviet state and the entire nation lovingly preserve the monuments of the past which elevate the human mind and broaden it to an awareness and appreciation of the beautiful.

Liudmila Ivanova

1. Entrance to Peterstadt

82. The Palace of Peter III. The north façade

83. The Upper Park. *Cupid*, 18th-century copy of the sculpture by Etienne-Maurice Falconet

84. The Palace of Peter III. The Study

85. The Picture Room

86. View of the Karost River

87. View of the Great Palace across the Lower Pond

88. The Upper Park. *Jonah*, decorative sculpture

89. The Upper Park. *Antinous*, 18th-century copy of an antique bust

90. View of the Chinese Palace across the Upper Pond

91. The Upper Park. Oak trees near the Chinese Palace

92. The Chinese Palace. The south façade

93. The Hall of the Muses

94. The Buglework Room

95. The Lilac Drawing Room

96. The Large Chinese Room

97. The Dressing Room

100. The Wardrobe Room

99. The Boudoir

98. The Entrance Hall

101. The Portrait Room

102. The Upper Park. The English Drive

103. The Upper Park. The Maple Walk

104. The Upper Park.
The Coasting Hill Pavilion

105. The Round Hall

106. The Porcelain Room

PAVLOVSK

The Pavlovsk complex is justly considered a gem among the Russian palace and park ensembles of the late eighteenth and early nineteenth centuries. The magic fountains of Peterhof had long begun to spout their waters, merry-making on the Coasting Hill at Oranienbaum was already in full swing, and Tsarskoye Selo had seen many a sumptuous celebration, when the wooded banks of the tranquil Slavianka, where Pavlovsk was to stand, were still only hunting grounds for the royal family.

The building of Pavlovsk was begun almost two hundred years ago, in 1777. It was conceived as a summer residence for Paul, the son of Catherine II, then heir apparent. In 1780 Pavlovsk saw the arrival of Charles Cameron, the architect who was to make an important contribution to the creation of the complex. He designed the Great Palace and many of the park pavilions, all built in 1782—86. Erected by 1786 was the central block of the Palace, with two symmetrical one-storey colonnaded galleries adjoined by wings one and a half storeys high. This design was typical of country mansions in the last quarter of the eighteenth century. At the end of the 1780s, supervision of the project passed into the hands of Vincenzo Brenna (1745—1820), who completed the work. In 1796, when Paul ascended the throne of Russia, Brenna was appointed Architect-in-Chief to the Court. He significantly enlarged the dimensions of the Palace by adding a second storey over the galleries and wings and erecting two new service blocks; he also decorated many of the state rooms. Brenna invited the well-known sculptors Ivan Martos, Mikhail Kozlovsky, and Ivan Prokofyev to work at Pavlovsk. The decorative painting was commissioned to Giovanni Scotti, Johann Mettenleiter, Andrey Martynov, and Pietro Gonzaga. The Throne Room, the Picture Gallery, the Church Gallery, the Chapel Royal, and other interiors were given a décor of stately magnificence, fully in keeping with the Palace's new role of an imperial residence.

In 1803 the decorative furnishings of the state rooms were seriously damaged in a fire. The reconstruction of the interiors was entrusted to Andrey Voronikhin (1760—1814), an outstanding Russian architect who was to serve as Chief Architect of Pavlovsk for many years. Voronikhin displayed the tact and discretion of a truly talented artist in adjusting his own individual style to accord with the creative manner of the masters who had preceded him. He not only revived the gutted halls, but designed the new furniture, lighting fixtures, and decorative vases as well. At almost the same time as Voronikhin, Giacomo Quarenghi was doing the décor of the rooms on the ground floor. The palace complex was brought to its completion in 1822—24 by one of the most talented architects of the time, Carlo Rossi (1775—1849). He designed and built the Palace Library and elaborated on the artistic finish of the interiors.

Pavlovsk

Notwithstanding the participation of as many as five architects in the construction and ornamentation of the palace, the Pavlovsk ensemble boasts an amazing stylistic unity. One of the reasons is that it was created in a period when Russian architecture was dominated by one style, that of Classicism, and like all the Classicists, the architects of Pavlovsk drew their inspiration, and borrowed their decorative devices, from the art of ancient Greece and Rome. But notwithstanding this unity of style, the work of each of the five at Pavlovsk bears a stamp of his artistic individuality. Another feature peculiar to the Pavlovsk Palace is that in all the subsequent years of its existence it was subjected to no significant alterations of any kind.

Pavlovsk is the repository of magnificent collections of paintings, antique sculptures, and works of decorative art by Russian and Western European masters. The Picture Gallery and other palace interiors are graced by the canvases of Italian, French, Dutch, and Flemish artists, such as Carlo Dolci, Guido Reni, Francesco Parmigianino, Francesco Albani, Luca Giordano, Charles Lebrun, Pierre Mignard, Peter Paul Rubens, Adriaen van Ostade, Jan van Goyen, Pieter Claesz, and many other sixteenth to eighteenth century artists. The works of Hubert Robert, Girolamo Battoni, Angelica Kauffmann, and Anton Raffael Mengs were executed by their authors on commissions from the owners of Pavlovsk. Various lighting fixtures, Gobelins tapestries, carved and gilded furniture and furniture of the rarer species of wood from the workshops of Henri Jacob, Pierre Denizot, and David Roentgen, precious decorative bronzes and porcelains — all these, for the greater part unique, works of art, placed in interiors finished with the utmost elegance and refinement, made Pavlovsk into what Anatoly Lunacharsky, an outstanding art critic and People's Commissar for Education in those days, called "a monument with but few equals in Europe."

The Palace is organically linked to the park and serves as its compositional pivot. Concurrently with the erection of the Great Palace, Charles Cameron, Vincenzo Brenna, and the decorator and landscape designer Pietro Gonzaga were working on the layout and landscaping of the Pavlovsk park, producing several distinct areas of inimitable beauty: the Great Star, Old Sylvia, New Sylvia, White Birch, the Slavianka Valley, the Valley of the Pools, and the Central or Palace Area. These seven main regions create seven poetic images of Russian nature. Alternating open and enclosed spaces, sheets of water and stretches of forest, classical structures and rustic pavilions, romantic ruins, light bridges, dams, an abundance of marble and bronze sculptures placed all over the park — all serve to give infinite artistic variety to the scene.

It is only natural, therefore, that after passing from private ownership into the hands of the people in 1917, the Pavlovsk Palace and Park complex should have become so popular.

Pavlovsk

In the beginning of the War of 1941—45, immediately after the Nazi onslaught, the art treasures of the palace museums in the environs of Leningrad were made ready for evacuation. Thousands of items were despatched inland. Even under the difficult conditions of the war the Soviet Government made every effort to preserve and protect the country's artistic heritage. The bulk of the Pavlovsk collections of paintings, porcelains, glass, bronze, and sculpture was saved only because it was evacuated in time. The antique sculptures and coloured stone vases from the Palace interiors were immured in caches made in its cellars, and the park sculptures were buried in the ground. The staff of the museum did all that was humanly possible to save the museum's treasures, displaying true heroism and an exemplary devotion to duty.

The palace building, however, suffered tremendous damage. The Hitlerites reduced it to a pile of ruins; they also plundered and destroyed the park pavilions, blew up the bridges, cut down seventy thousand trees and thirty thousand bushes. All told, the damage inflicted on Pavlovsk by Nazi troops is estimated at several million roubles.

In January 1944 Pavlovsk was liberated from Nazi occupation. The guns of war were still roaring when preservation work was set afoot: the skeleton of the palace was cleared of rubble, the surviving fragments of the ornamental details and furnishings were reinforced and provided with protective covering. Confident that all the wounds of wartime would be healed, the staff of the Pavlovsk museum set to work to resurrect one of the country's finest architectural and artistic monuments. The timely evacuation, which had saved most of the furnishings, greatly facilitated the restoration of the palace's interiors to their former aspect after the reconstruction of the edifice itself had been completed.

The first seven interiors, among them the Church Gallery and the Throne Room, were opened to the public in June 1957; the Picture Gallery and three lobbies in the following year; the next to be restored and displayed to visitors was the private suite of the ground floor. In April 1970, on the eve of the centenary of the birth of Lenin and twenty-five years after the beginning of restoration work, the last eight rooms, all on the ground floor of the main building, were brought to completion and opened to visitors. In all, there are in the palace forty-five interiors whose decorative finish has been fully restored.

Taking part in the rebuilding of the Pavlovsk Palace Museum were many design, construction, and restoration firms in Leningrad. The methods of restoration employed were worked out by the Science department of the Pavlovsk Museum. The decorative painting of the walls and ceilings has been recreated in twenty-eight palace interiors. All the ornate stucco mouldings, the elegant ornamental and figure carving, the sculpture, relief decoration, and the gilding were

Pavlovsk

executed by talented masters who received their artistic training in special vocational and art schools. Bricklayers and marble-cutters, carpenters and parquet makers, plasterers and house-painters, metalworkers, electricians, and heating technicians (the list could be continued indefinitely) — these are the specialists whose work went into the rebuilding of the Pavlovsk Palace. No less important was the contribution of those who recreated the furnishings. The restoration of the Palace has by and large been brought to completion. It remains only for the Gonzaga Gallery to be decorated and the last articles of furniture to be reproduced for the Pavlovsk Palace to assume its original eighteenth century aspect.

Major restoration work has also been conducted in the park. Newly planted trees and shrubs have replaced those cut down during the war. The Apollo Colonnade, the Temple to Friendship, and the Peel Tower have been restored, and the restoration of the Monument to the Parents and the Music Pavilion is nearing completion. Repair work on Paul's Mausoleum will soon begin. The foundation has been laid of the Rose Pavilion which is to be reconstructed as a monument to the glory of Russian arms; the bridges have been rebuilt and the roads repaired. Large-scale work is under way in the White Birch area.

Visitors from many cities of the Soviet Union and foreign guests alike speak highly of the work done by the restorers at Pavlovsk, which has once again become one of the most widely visited parks of the country.

Valeria Belanina

108. The Grecian Hall

107. The Palace

109. The Hall of Peace

110. The Italian Hall

111. The Dressing Room

112. The Library of the northern suite

113. The Library of the southern suite

114. The First Anteroom

115. The Throne Room

116. The Picture Gallery

117. The Church Gallery

118. The Old Drawing Room

119. View of the Centaur Bridge and the Cold Baths Pavilion

120. View of the Palace across the Slavianka River

121. One of the Great Circles (parterres)

122. The Aviary. View across the pond

123. The Apollo Colonnade

124. The Pavilion of the Three Graces

125. The Great Stone Stairway

126. View of the Temple to Friendship

127. *Rond point* at the crossing of the Twelve Walks. Winter scene

128. *Melpomene*, sculpture in the *rond point* at the crossing of the Twelve Walks

129. The Peel Tower

130. The Ruin Bridge

131. The Slavianka, with the Visconti Bridge in the distance

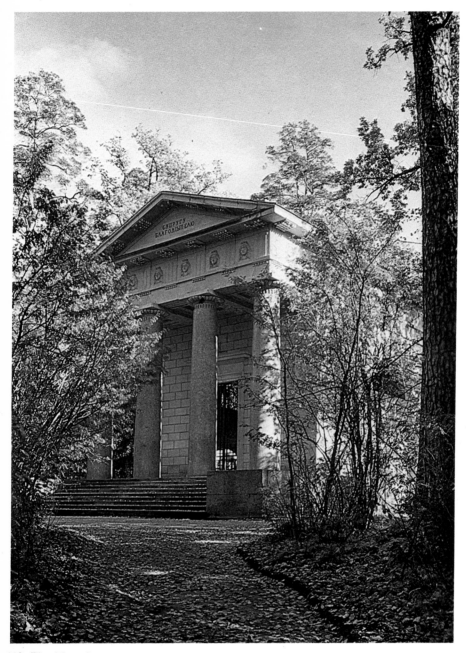

132. The Mausoleum

133. A walk in the New Sylvia

134. View in the White Birch Area

135. View of a walk in the park

REPINO

The last ten years have seen the virtual transformation of the Karelian Isthmus. The northern coast of the Gulf of Finland is today studded with multi-storey boarding houses, sanatoria, hotels, and rest and work homes for writers, actors, painters and other creative artists. Only one small plot of ground at the 45th kilometre of the Maritime Highway has not been affected. Just as at the turn of the century, every person who walks or drives by cannot fail to notice a low wooden gate leading into a park where, partly hidden by trees, stands a house with a lantern on the roof, several verandas, and balconies. This is The Penates, once the home of the well-known Russian artist Ilya Efimovich Repin (1844—1930).

Repin purchased the house and grounds in 1899, but moved in for good only in 1903. In the course of these years Repin himself planned and supervised the construction of a number of annexes, and the weed-grown, marshy plot was transformed into a small picturesque park with ponds, quaint summerhouses, and shady walks. All that was undertaken here served to create the maximum of comfort, and the most congenial atmosphere, for the work to which Repin dedicated his whole life.

When Repin moved from St Petersburg to The Penates at Kuokkala, he was a famous artist very much in the public eye. He was well liked also for his patronage of young talents. His passion for literature and music, and his deep respect for men of science, attracted to The Penates artists, writers, musicians and scientists alike. The house played host to the writers Maxim Gorky, Vladimir Mayakovsky, Sergey Esenin, Ivan Bunin, Alexander Kuprin, the scientists Vladimir Bekhterev, Ivan Tarkhanov, Ivan Pavlov, and many others. That is why we cherish The Penates as a memorial, not only to the great artist himself, but also to the outstanding representatives of early twentieth century Russian culture, who regularly visited here.

Repin nourished the hope that after his death The Penates would become a centre where artists could come and work, a museum that would attract all those who were interested in Russian art. He willed The Penates to the Academy of Arts, but a long time was to pass before that will could be implemented: for over two decades The Penates was separated from Russia, and it was only in 1939 that the place was converted into a memorial museum. When at the

Repino

end of the War of 1941—45 the Soviet Army liberated the Karelian Isthmus, Repin's house had been reduced to a heap of ashes surrounded by charred trees; the park had thinned significantly, the ponds were overgrown with moss and osiers, and the summerhouses were no more. In 1944, on the centenary of Repin's birth, the Soviet Government authorized the rebuilding of The Penates and renamed Kuokkala, Repino. By 1962 The Penates had reassumed its aspect of 1905—14, when its construction had been, by and large, completed. Like the Pushkin memorial home of Mikhailovskoye and Lev Tolstoy's of Yasnaya Poliana, like the Chekhov house in Yalta and the Chaikovsky in Klin, The Penates is a Russian national cultural monument.

Tours of The Penates generally begin with the three rooms where large photo reproductions of Repin's most important works hang on the walls, and photocopies of various documents and letters, and documentary photographs, are displayed in the showcases. These materials serve to remind the visitor of the principal stages in Repin's creative career and allow him to observe the evolution of the artist's talent.

The Raising of Jairus's Daughter was Repin's first major picture, which won him a gold medal upon graduation from the Academy of Arts. Many of the finest works of the artist's creative legacy, — such as *Barge Haulers on the Volga, Religious Procession in the Province of Kursk, A Send-off for the Recruit,* — lay bare the social contradictions of his time. Pictures like *They Did Not Expect Him, Spurning the Confession,* and *The Arrest of a Propagandist* present dramatic episodes in the life of Russian revolutionaries, a life of selfless struggle for the happiness of the people. Canvases like *Ivan the Terrible and His Son Ivan* were perceived by Repin's contemporaries as a veiled reflection of modern events in historical themes. In his portraits of writers, artists, scientists, and composers Repin sought not only to render the individual features of his sitters with the utmost exactitude, but to convey the innermost workings of their souls as well. We may mention as examples his portraits of Tolstoy, Moussorgsky, Stasov, and Strepetova.

Among the documents on display there are some which relate to the last years of the artist's life. He spent these away from Soviet Russia, and was delighted whenever he received tidings from his native land. In a showcase by the window are some of the books sent to Repin by friends in the Soviet Union, including works by Lenin and Lunacharsky. In 1926 a delegation of artists from Russia — Isaak Brodsky, Pavel Radimov, Eugene Katzman and Alexander Grigoryev — called on Repin and on behalf of the Soviet Government offered him an invitation to come back home. Much as he wished to, however, the old man, then eighty-two, feeble and alone (his children were opposed to their father's repatriation), was unable to avail himself of the opportunity.

The memorial rooms — Repin's studio and study, the parlour, dining-room and entrance hall — have been reconstructed after old photographs. On display here are those personal relics of the artist which survived the war. Some of the furniture pieces are authentic, others are duplicates (identical items purchased from private owners), still others are replicas, like the dining-room table reproduced from old designs; but all conform strictly to their prototypes of Repin's day, as documented by contemporary photographs and drawings of the interiors. There are over a hundred of Repin's own pictures in oils and graphic works in these rooms, as well as works by his talented pupils, later well-known painters, Philip Maliavin, Isaak Brodsky, Boris Kustodiev, and Ivan Kulikov.

The memorial exhibition begins with the modest entrance hall. Hanging on the rack is the artist's black hooded cloak and broad-brimmed hat, and in a corner are two walking-sticks and an old iron shovel he liked to use in the garden. The famous gong — a copper disc on a bamboo stand — is near the window, and over it is a cardboard placard with the words: "Self-help. Take off your coats and galoshes yourself. Open the door into the dining-room yourself..." Self-help was the motto of Repin's household — the servants were not supposed to wait on anyone, and the guests had to manage for themselves. Repin always considered personal attendance degrading and incompatible with human dignity. Standing just beside the front door in the entrance hall is the old, once light blue, flag of The Penates, with the word ПЕНАТЫ painted in black. It used to be raised over the house regularly every Wednesday to signify that the owners were at home and receiving.

Repino

We proceed next to the study, which was the last annex to the house. This room has a curved wall whose upper part is all window. It is always flooded with light. Here, sitting at his writing table, Repin loved to draw and to answer numerous letters; here, too, he wrote his *Reminiscences*. The tops of the low bookshelves lining the curved wall are graced by Ilya Ginzburg's sculptured portraits of Dmitry Mendeleyev, Vladimir Stasov, Anatoly Koni, Vasily Surikov, Leo Tolstoy and Anton Rubinstein. On the writing table are photographs of Repin's parents, relatives, and friends, and also a briefcase, a paper weight, a large magnifying glass mounted into the lid of a special case, a reading lamp, two candlesticks, and other objects used by the artist.

Repin was one of the most widely educated artists of his time. He was a voracious reader, and liked to discuss with others the books he had read. Deeply interested in the most diverse fields of knowledge, he had an immense admiration for the achievements of science. Repin's library is full of books autographed by scientists and writers, artists and musicians. The writer Korney Chukovsky once rightly said about Repin that "all his life he lived on the summits of culture." In his last years he eagerly read books by Soviet authors and marvelled in his letters at the giftedness of young Russian writers. At eighty-two Repin evinced a serious interest in the works of Lenin sent to him from Russia at his request. Here, in this study, in the 1920s, Repin used to listen to broadcasts from the Soviet Union over a little crystal receiver.

Music and the theatre were one of Repin's most ardent loves. Many outstanding musicians and actors were personal friends of the artist and willingly came to The Penates. There was a piano in the parlour and always some music books on it. Fiodor Shaliapin and Ivan Ershov sang here, Alexander Glazunov and Boris Asafyev performed their works, and this chamber also heard the music of Sergey Rakhmaninov and Alexander Skriabin. Sometimes, in the summer, there were so many guests that the improvised concerts had to be carried over into the park.

There were special albums in the house where guests left their autographs, notes, drawings or verses. A sheet from one of the albums (on the grand piano in the parlour) carries, among other things, a cartoon of Tsar Nicholas II by the artist Valery Carrick, and underneath, in Maxim Gorky's hand, the words "Who is this freak?" Repin's antimonarchist views and his

Repino

sympathy with the revolution of 1905—7 are recorded in his letters; he also planned several canvases devoted to the events of that period — *The Dispersal of a Demonstration, The 17th of October 1905, A Red Funeral,* and others. Repin presented his sketches for these pictures to the Soviet Union in 1926; today they are housed in the Museum of the Revolution in Moscow.

The parlour was sometimes referred to as the Venus Room because one of its features is a plaster cast of the antique statue of Venus of Milo. There is also an early Repin here — a portrait in watercolours of the architect Petrov, and a number of works by Repin's pupils — a dog study by Valentin Serov, a portrait of Chukovsky and a landscape by Brodsky, a landscape by Alexander Skalon, and a smal-size self-portrait in watercolours of Repin's first wife, Vera Shevtsova. Also deserving of interest are several portraits by painters from the town of Chuguyev, who were Repin's first teachers.

From the parlour there is a door to the glassed winter veranda which during Repin's first years at The Penates served as his painting studio. The artist was also fond of sculpting, and there is a special stand for modelling here, and busts executed by Repin of Leo Tolstoy, Natalya Nordman-Severova, the artist's second wife, the surgeon Nikolay Pirogov, as well as one of young Repin himself (1880) — the only sculptured work ever done by his friend, the painter Victor Vasnetsov. On June 5, 1905 Repin, Stasov and others heard Gorky read his play *Children of the Sun,* only just completed. This event was depicted by Repin in a drawing, a reproduction of which hangs on the door jamb at the entrance to the veranda.

Another door leads from the parlour to the famous dining-room of The Penates, with its round table. The central raised part of the table revolved freely so that guests could help themselves to any dish they liked without assistance. The humorous *Rules of the Round Table* prohibited guests from asking for the help of any of their table companions, including the hosts. Anybody who broke that rule had to mount a specially erected rostrum in the corner and deliver an impromptu speech on one of the burning issues of the day. In the decade between 1905 and 1914 the round table saw many a gathering of the flower of progressive Russian intelligentsia, among them Vladimir Mayakovsky, Anatoly Koni, Sergey Gorodetsky, Vladimir Korolenko,

Repino

Isaak Brodsky, Igor Grabar, Leonid Andreyev, Velemir Khlebnikov, and many others. The walls of the dining-room are decorated with Repin's pictures and studies. Unfortunately, much of The Penates collection was sold abroad in the artist's lifetime. The greater part of his artistic legacy, however, was disposed of by the artist's children after his death. Of the surviving works, mention should be made of a portrait of Nordman (painted at Fasano in 1905), a pastel portrait of the actor Grigory Gay, a portrait of Repin's daughters Vera and Nadia, and a pungent graphic portrait (1926) of Vera Repina, that unhappy influence in Repin's life and in the fate which befell his artistic legacy.

The most important part of the house was the studio where Repin painted his pictures. This so-called winter studio occupies two thirds of the upper floor. It could be converted into three separate workshops by drawing the draperies across. Repin liked to have several pictures going at a time. His pupils could work here too without getting in his way.

Repin toiled from morning to late evening. "In the mornings, immediately after breakfast," reminisces Chukovsky, "he hurried to the studio and there literally worked himself to exhaustion in the creative process, because he was a toiler beyond compare and was even slightly ashamed of the passion which drove him to work, never once relinquishing the brush, from dawn to dusk, and made him utterly spend himself on the huge canvases which surrounded him in the studio . . ." In the 1890s, when Repin's right hand began to fail because of incessant toil, he took to painting with his left. It was then that he devised a special palette to be worn at the belt. This palette is now on display in the winter studio, along with his easel, brushes, and other art equipment.

Here, in the winter studio of The Penates, Repin painted the portraits of the writers Korolenko and Chukovsky and the historian Nikolay Kareyev. There were some themes to which the artist returned after a lapse of many years, as, for instance, that of Zaporozhye Cossacks. Long after the creation of his famous canvas *The Zaporozhye Cossacks Writing a Mocking Letter to the Turkish Sultan*, Repin elaborated on the subject in The Penates in the pictures *Free Warriors of the Black Sea Coast* and *The Gopak* (a folk dance). On display at the studio are the costumes for the models, some Zaporozhian artifacts (a bandore, a match-lock gun, swords, and saddlebags), which Repin used for pictures, and, finally, figurines of the Cossacks sculpted by Repin himself for use in compositional sketches.

One of the gems of The Penates' collection is a sketch in oils for *The State Council in Session*. It is accompanied by several studies for the picture, executed by Repin and his pupils, Kustodiev and Kulikov, who assisted the master in his work. The painted self-portrait of 1920 is an exceptionally valuable exhibit because it captured for posterity the image of Repin in his old age, a lonely man and sad. The brushes and the palette which he introduced into the canvas symbolize painting, the love of his life, so that the caption to the portrait could well have been the words Repin wrote in one of his letters: "Above all, I have not abandoned art. My last thoughts are all about Art."

From the winter studio one can go up two flights of steps to the artist's summer workshop, which today houses an exhibition of drawings by Repin, his pupils, and his friends. The windows of both workshops overlook the park with its ponds and shady alleys. Water for these ponds flowed from an artesian well, of which Repin was particularly proud.

Repin's grave is situated on a low mound in the depths of the park. He chose the place himself. Shortly before his death the artist wrote: "Now from my window I can always see my future grave between two junipers which so resemble cypresses."

The Penates is visited by scores of thousands of persons annually. In the twelve years of the museum's existence it has had over a million and a half visitors. People come from Leningrad, from all parts of the Soviet Union, and from abroad because they are attracted to the place where the great realist artist lived, worked, and is buried, an artist whose works are the pride of the Russian people yet belong to the whole civilized world.

Elena Levenfish

136. Repin's Memorial Home, The Penates

137. View of the house across the pond

138. Entrance gate of The Penates

139. Entrance hall

140. Repin's study

141. The parlour

142. The parlour

143. The dining-room

144. The winter veranda

145. The winter studio

146. The winter studio. Repin's collection of Zaporozhian artifacts

147. The park. Pavilion "Temple of Osiris and Isis"

148. View in the park

149. Repin's tomb

CONTENTS

**PLACES OF INTEREST
IN THE ENVIRONS OF LENINGRAD**
Historical and Architectural Monuments

**ДОСТОПРИМЕЧАТЕЛЬНОСТИ
ПРИГОРОДОВ ЛЕНИНГРАДА**

*Путеводитель по историко-мемориальным местам
и дворцам-музеям*

*Фотографии М. А. Величко, Б. В. Манушина,
В. И. Савика, В. А. Стукалова*
Оформление художника Б. Н. Осенчакова
Перевод с русского языка Ю. И. Немецкого
Редактор Д. А. Алексеева
Художественный редактор А. Р. Шилов
Редактор английского текста Л. Я. Сорокина
Технический редактор Н. А. Зубкова
Корректор В. А. Фатеев

Подписано в печать 7/VIII 1973. Формат 70×84 1/16,
бумага мелованная. Усл. печ. л. 15,53
Уч.-изд. л. 15,09. Изд. № 1653. (8-13). Заказ 9011
Издательство «Аврора». 191065, Ленинград, Невский пр., 7/9
Издано в СССР